INVENTIONS & DISCOVERIES

*English edition translated from the Italian
and edited by Maureen Spurgeon*

Brown Watson

ENGLAND

Production: Cristina Drago

Editors: Daniela Majerna, Stefano Sibella
Editorial Assistant: Maria Pia Arciuli

Text: Bianca Venturi
Scientific Consultant: Ugo Scaioni
Graphics: Vittorino Monzini
Art and Design: Gabriele Clima, Graffito s.r.l.

Contents

First Discoveries 4

From Heat To Movement 6

Electric Light 8

Laser Beams 10

Revealing The Invisible 12

Beyond 'The Naked Eye' 14

'Recording' The Image 16

Long Distance Communication 18

A 'Magic' Box 20

Books For All 22

'Intelligent' Machines 24

The Passage Of Time 26

Antibiotics and Vaccines 28

'Made To Measure' Organisms 30

Glossary 32

FIRST DISCOVERIES

Using their natural intelligence, our earliest ancestors soon learned to use the materials and objects close at hand in ways to help them. The discovery of fire, the moulding of metals, the use of animals, the development of farming and the invention of the wheel – all these marked the first great changes in the story of civilization. With the Industrial Revolution in the 1800s, 'man-powered' machines were quickly improved and perfected, leading to the development of new technology in our lifetime. It is humankind's constant quest for discovery that has resulted in astronauts overcoming the boundaries of Earth in the conquest of space.

Fire

The first fires were probably caused by lightning. People must have seen the same sort of sparks flashing as they worked, and this probably gave them the idea of rubbing two stones or two pieces of wood together, to make fire. And with fire, they could keep warm, cook food and harden the points of wooden spears.

spear

Metals

Metals were first worked 'cold'. Then, from about 4500 BC, metals were melted by fire then cooled into shape in moulds. Fire was also used to shape metals such as bronze. From 1500 BC, iron began to be used to make arrow-heads and weapons.

Pulley

Invented by the Greeks in about 400 BC, this is a simple machine used for raising weights and for drawing water up from wells.

Pottery

Pottery was already in use 11,000 years before Christ. The first objects were made by modelling and kneading clay, then baking it until it was hard. By using a lathe (probably invented in 6500 BC in Asia Minor), potters could make containers in circular shapes.

Writing

Towards 3200 BC, the Sumerians carved picture symbols or drawings into clay, with each picture representing a word.

arrow-head made of flint

bow and arrow

fire

point of spear hardening in the fire

Cart

In about 3500 BC, Sumerians combined the invention of the wheel with a domesticated animal for pulling the first carts.

Archimedes' Screw

This machine dates from 250 BC. It was probably invented by the Greek scientist Archimedes. A handle turns a spiral inside a tube which scoops water up from a depth. It is still used in some parts of the world.

Coins

The first coins were exchanged in trading, taking the place of bargaining one object for another. Coins were first used by the Chinese around 700 BC.

FROM HEAT TO MOVEMENT

There are many types of engines according to the type of energy they use to make mechanical energy. For example – the internal combustion engine, like the one inside a car, or a turbine, burns fuel which gives off heat. This heat is converted into mechanical energy to make parts of the car move. With the coming of the Industrial Revolution in the 1800s, the first steam engines were improved and developed, then used in lots of different ways. Since those days, engines have supported the work of people and animals in transport and in industrial and agricultural applications.

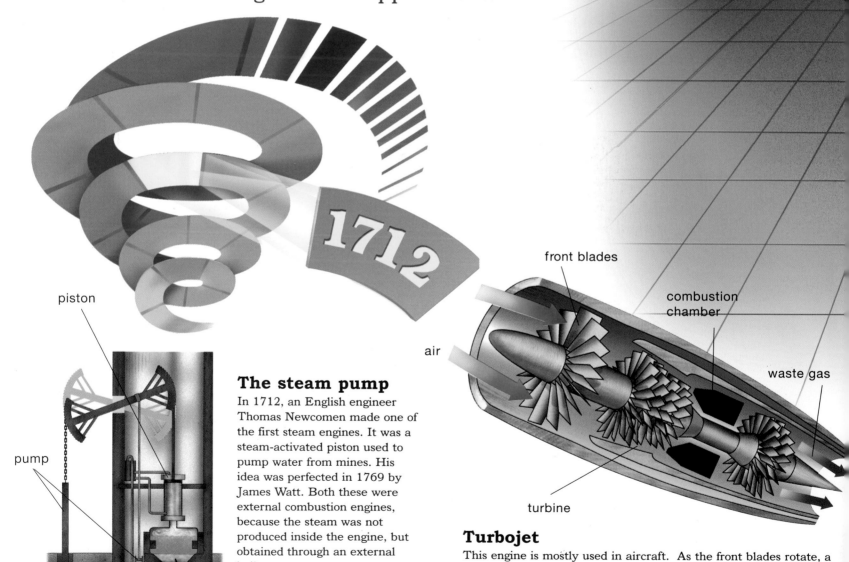

piston

pump

boiler

front blades

combustion chamber

air

waste gas

turbine

The steam pump

In 1712, an English engineer Thomas Newcomen made one of the first steam engines. It was a steam-activated piston used to pump water from mines. His idea was perfected in 1769 by James Watt. Both these were external combustion engines, because the steam was not produced inside the engine, but obtained through an external boiler.

Turbojet

This engine is mostly used in aircraft. As the front blades rotate, a compressor draws air into the engine and pushes it towards the combustion chamber, where fuel (usually kerosene) is burned. The gas produced from this combustion works a turbine which moves the rear blades, with exhaust gases discharged at great speed from the rear part of the engine. The force of this discharge gives the aircraft an upward thrust. This type of engine is called a reactor engine.

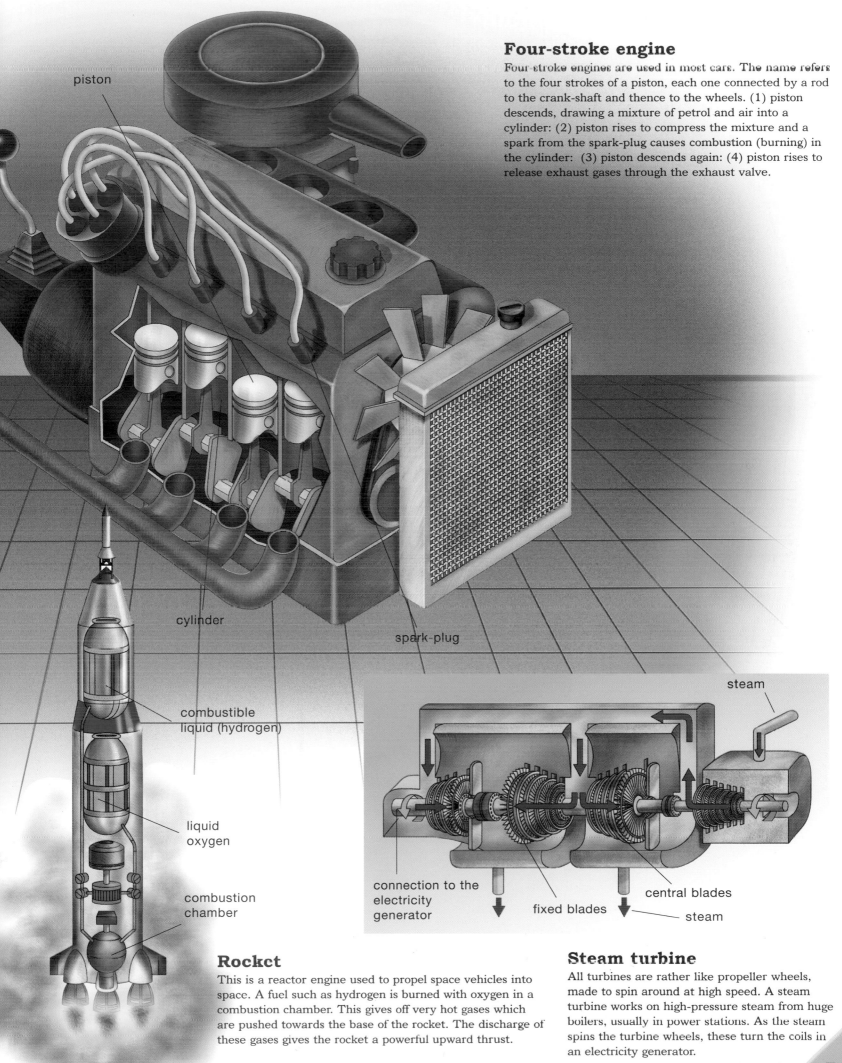

piston

Four-stroke engine

Four-stroke engines are used in most cars. The name refers to the four strokes of a piston, each one connected by a rod to the crank-shaft and thence to the wheels. (1) piston descends, drawing a mixture of petrol and air into a cylinder: (2) piston rises to compress the mixture and a spark from the spark-plug causes combustion (burning) in the cylinder: (3) piston descends again: (4) piston rises to release exhaust gases through the exhaust valve.

cylinder

spark-plug

steam

combustible liquid (hydrogen)

liquid oxygen

combustion chamber

connection to the electricity generator

fixed blades

central blades

steam

Rocket

This is a reactor engine used to propel space vehicles into space. A fuel such as hydrogen is burned with oxygen in a combustion chamber. This gives off very hot gases which are pushed towards the base of the rocket. The discharge of these gases gives the rocket a powerful upward thrust.

Steam turbine

All turbines are rather like propeller wheels, made to spin around at high speed. A steam turbine works on high-pressure steam from huge boilers, usually in power stations. As the steam spins the turbine wheels, these turn the coils in an electricity generator.

ELECTRIC LIGHT

The discovery of electricity led to many inventions, such as the electric light bulb. This works by the transformation of electrical energy into light energy through the heating up of a thin wire. The main problem was finding a wire (the filament) that would not burn too quickly and so give out light for a long enough time.

1879

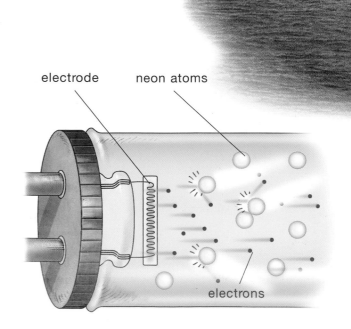

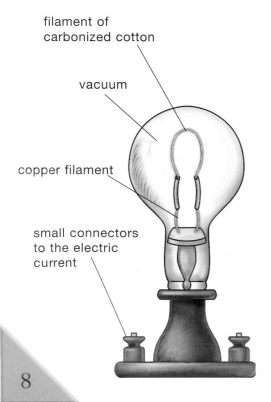

filament of carbonized cotton

vacuum

copper filament

small connectors to the electric current

Edison's light bulb

In 1880 the first electric light bulb was independently produced by Joseph Wilson Swan in England and by Thomas Alva Edison in the USA. Edison used a thread of fine, carbonized cotton sealed into a glass bulb from which all the air had been taken out and placed upside down. When an electric current was passed through the bulb, the cotton filament glowed brightly, but it did not burn because there was no oxygen.

electrode   neon atoms

electrons

Electric light bulb

Light inside a bulb is produced partly from the metal tungsten filament and partly from an inert (non-moving) gas which will not make the filament burn. The bulb is connected to the electrical circuit by a metal fitting.

inert gas

nickel electrode

tungsten filament

connection (fitting)

Neon light bulb

This gives out light when the electrons produced by an electrical discharge bombard atoms of neon, all enclosed in a glass tube. Different colours are obtained by mixing or adding other types of gas to the neon. This effect is used for luminous signs.

Halogen light bulb

As well as inert gas, this type of light bulb also contains halogen gases, such as iodine and bromide, which lengthen the life of the tungsten filament.

9

LASER BEAMS

The laser is a device which produces a beam of very intense light, in the form of a light wave which is equal in length, frequency and direction. The name comes from the initials of the words Light Amplification by Stimulated Emission of Radiation. The laser can amplify (make more powerful) light generated within it into a beam which is so strong and precise that it can travel for thousands of kilometres without weakening, concentrating energy precisely at a given point, or cutting neatly through thick sheets of steel.

1960

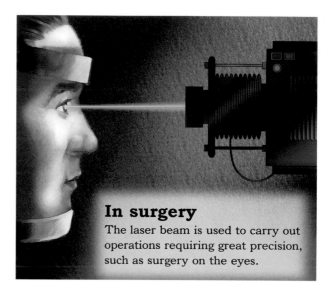

In surgery
The laser beam is used to carry out operations requiring great precision, such as surgery on the eyes.

The first laser
American physicist Theodore Maiman built the first laser in 1960. This consisted of a cylindrical crystal of synthetic (man-made) ruby with a mirror at each end. A burst of intense light made the chromium atoms in the ruby send out a red light. This light was reflected back and forth between the mirrors, until it became an intense beam of laser light, so powerful that it blocked out sunlight. The importance of the discovery was only fully understood many years later. Today the laser is used in many ways.

At the supermarket
At a cash register, a laser beam is first reflected from a mirror and then a holographic disc to 'strike' the product being bought and to 'read' the bar code. This disc reflects the rays to a scanner which converts the optical signals into electrical impulses and then feeds the information into a computer. The computer identifies the goods being bought and supplies the price to the cash desk.

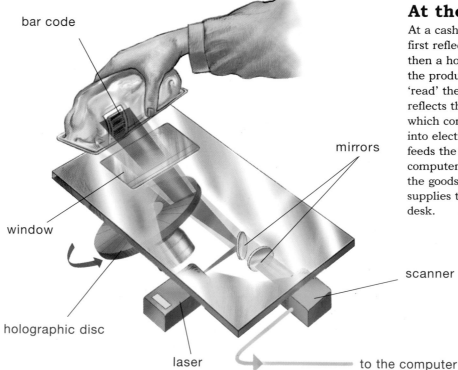

bar code

mirrors

window

holographic disc

laser

scanner

to the computer

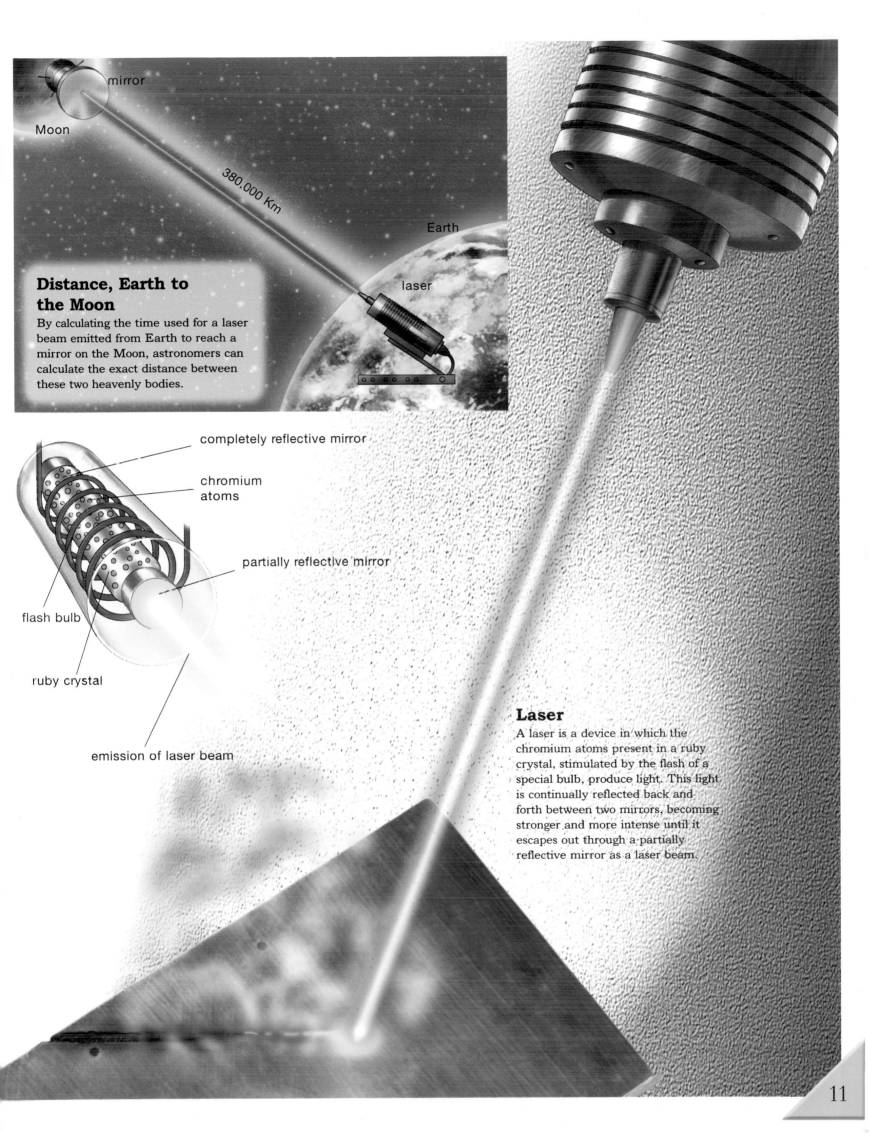

Distance, Earth to the Moon

By calculating the time used for a laser beam emitted from Earth to reach a mirror on the Moon, astronomers can calculate the exact distance between these two heavenly bodies.

mirror

Moon

380.000 Km

Earth

laser

completely reflective mirror

chromium atoms

partially reflective mirror

flash bulb

ruby crystal

emission of laser beam

Laser

A laser is a device in which the chromium atoms present in a ruby crystal, stimulated by the flash of a special bulb, produce light. This light is continually reflected back and forth between two mirrors, becoming stronger and more intense until it escapes out through a partially reflective mirror as a laser beam.

REVEALING THE INVISIBLE

X-rays are electromagnetic waves. They are rather like radio and light waves, but much shorter and therefore more penetrating. They can go through soft body tissue, but they are blocked by the harder parts – that is, the bone – and this makes clear shadows on a photographic film. X-rays can be put to many uses – in medicine, to discover the fracture of a bone, and in physics and chemistry, to study the structure of crystals or the molecules of a compound. In the restoration of works of art, X-rays can even reveal forgery, by using techniques such as measuring the density of the brush strokes of any one artist.

1895

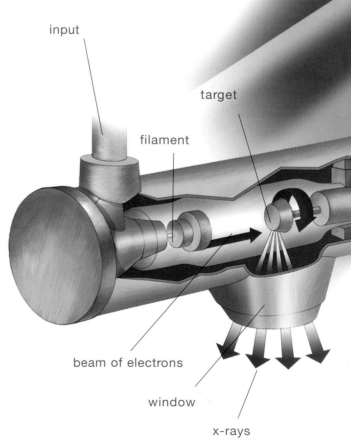

input

target

filament

beam of electrons

window

x-rays

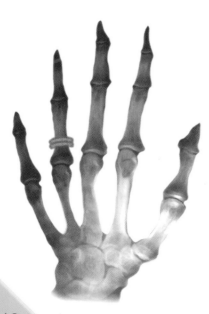

The first radiograph

In 1895, during experiments on the effects of a flow of electrons, the German physicist Wilhelm Röntgen discovered an unknown kind of radiation. It was invisible, yet capable of going through dense matter and leaving an impression on a photographic plate. Knowing nothing about these new rays, he called them 'X-rays' using the sign for the unknown. One of the first radiographs was the hand of his wife Bertha, showing the bones and her ring.

X-rays

A filament of very hot metal produces and sends electrons against a target, which is also made of metal. The metal atoms hit by the electrons give off X-rays.

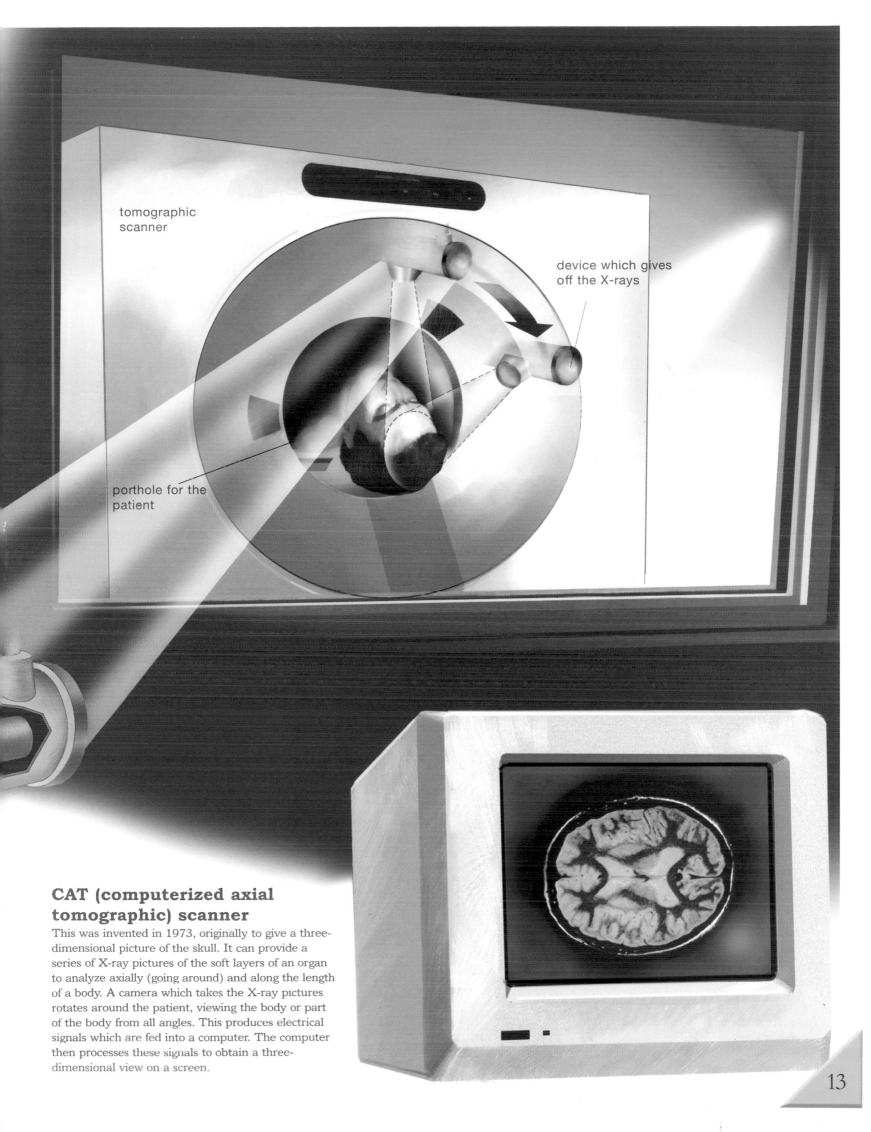

tomographic
scanner

device which gives
off the X-rays

porthole for the
patient

CAT (computerized axial tomographic) scanner

This was invented in 1973, originally to give a three-dimensional picture of the skull. It can provide a series of X-ray pictures of the soft layers of an organ to analyze axially (going around) and along the length of a body. A camera which takes the X-ray pictures rotates around the patient, viewing the body or part of the body from all angles. This produces electrical signals which are fed into a computer. The computer then processes these signals to obtain a three-dimensional view on a screen.

BEYOND 'THE NAKED EYE'

We see something when rays of light from the Sun or a light bulb hit an object and then are reflected back to our eyes. But the naked eye cannot see things which are too small or too far away. That is why optical instruments are needed. These use mirrors or lenses (sometimes both together) which direct the rays of light, either to enlarge an image (as with the microscope or telescope) or to make things clearer (as with spectacles).

solar panels

1609

Hubble space telescope

This telescope has been in orbit around the Earth since 1990. It works using two mirrors, each one only about 2 metres in diameter. These are able to view and take photographs around the Earth's atmosphere, providing information on heavenly bodies and astronomical events far away in outer space, and in time, such as the formation of new galaxies. The telescope's instruments are powered by solar panels.

Galileo's telescope

The first telescope for seeing distant objects was built in 1608 by a Dutch manufacturer of spectacles, Hans Lippershey. The following year, the Italian physicist and astronomer Galileo Galilei perfected a system of lenses to make the first astronomical telescope, so clear and powerful that he could use it to observe the mountains of the Moon and the satellites of the planet Jupiter.

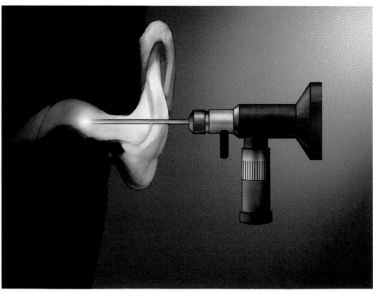

Otoscope

This is an instrument used in medicine. It works by a system of mirrors, like a little telescope. This enables a doctor to examine the ear from outside and to carry out surgical operations.

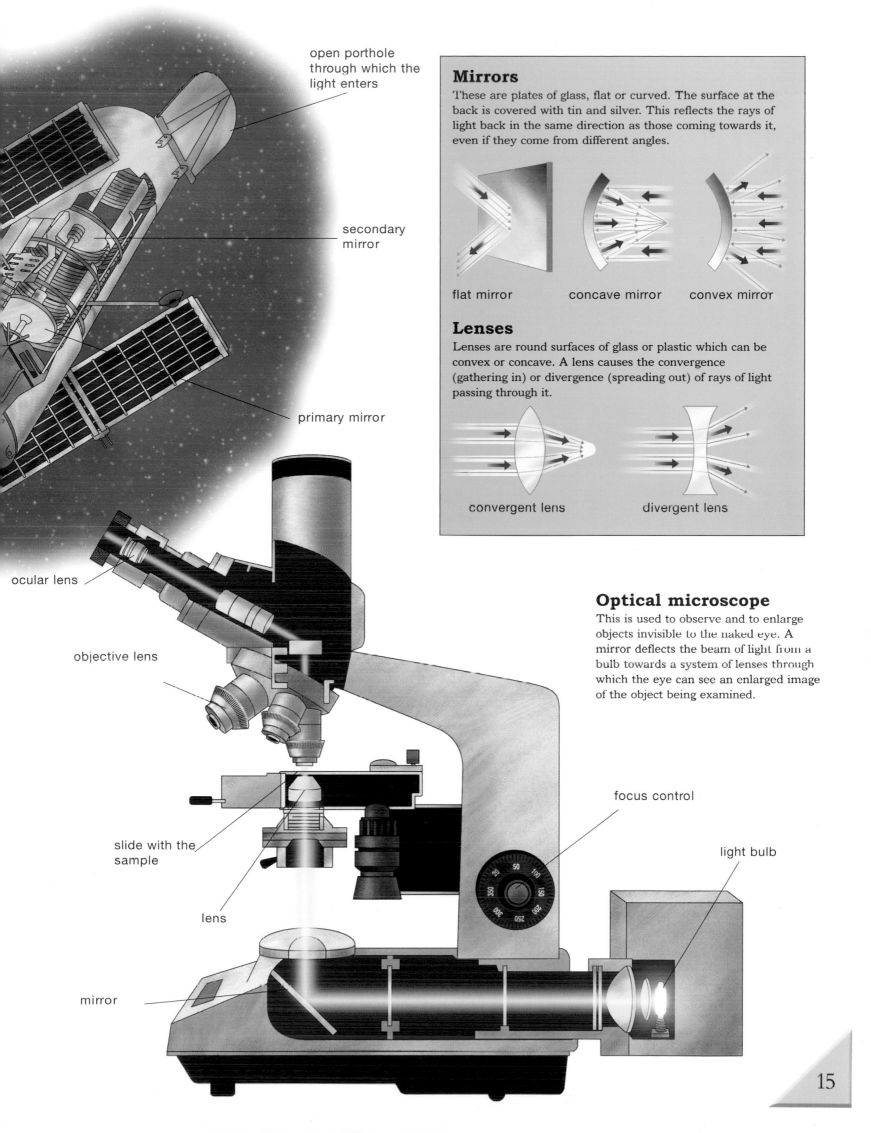

open porthole through which the light enters

secondary mirror

primary mirror

Mirrors

These are plates of glass, flat or curved. The surface at the back is covered with tin and silver. This reflects the rays of light back in the same direction as those coming towards it, even if they come from different angles.

flat mirror   concave mirror   convex mirror

Lenses

Lenses are round surfaces of glass or plastic which can be convex or concave. A lens causes the convergence (gathering in) or divergence (spreading out) of rays of light passing through it.

convergent lens   divergent lens

ocular lens

objective lens

Optical microscope

This is used to observe and to enlarge objects invisible to the naked eye. A mirror deflects the beam of light from a bulb towards a system of lenses through which the eye can see an enlarged image of the object being examined.

slide with the sample

focus control

lens

light bulb

mirror

'RECORDING' THE IMAGE

Photography is a chemical-physical process which enables us to record images, using light and an optical apparatus – the photographic machine. An ordinary camera works rather like a dark room – a black space where, through a small hole in one side, the light projected from an object outside penetrates and projects an image upside down. This photographic image is impressed on to a film which is sensitive to light, but 'in negative', with the clear areas appearing black and vice versa. So, the film has to be printed 'in positive' on special paper. This is also done by using light, through a process called 'development'.

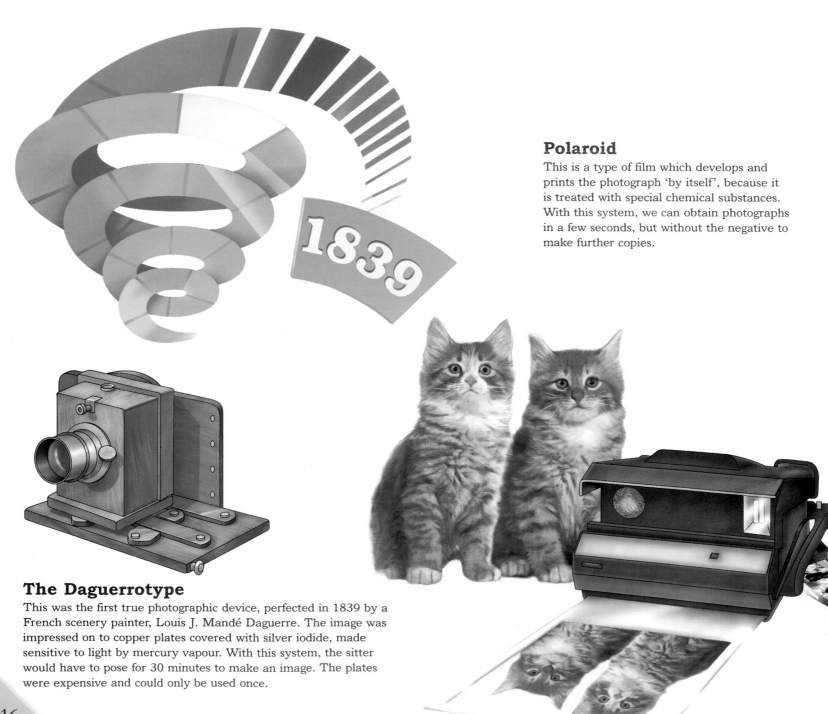

Polaroid
This is a type of film which develops and prints the photograph 'by itself', because it is treated with special chemical substances. With this system, we can obtain photographs in a few seconds, but without the negative to make further copies.

The Daguerrotype
This was the first true photographic device, perfected in 1839 by a French scenery painter, Louis J. Mandé Daguerre. The image was impressed on to copper plates covered with silver iodide, made sensitive to light by mercury vapour. With this system, the sitter would have to pose for 30 minutes to make an image. The plates were expensive and could only be used once.

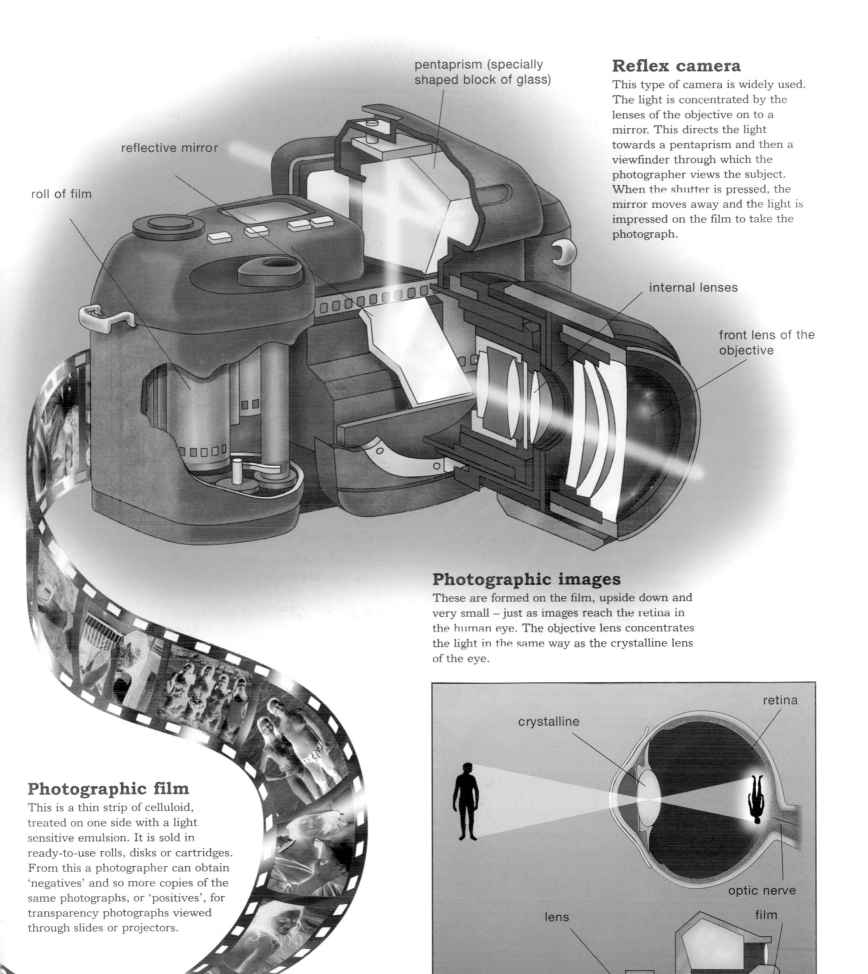

pentaprism (specially shaped block of glass)

reflective mirror

roll of film

Reflex camera

This type of camera is widely used. The light is concentrated by the lenses of the objective on to a mirror. This directs the light towards a pentaprism and then a viewfinder through which the photographer views the subject. When the shutter is pressed, the mirror moves away and the light is impressed on the film to take the photograph.

internal lenses

front lens of the objective

Photographic images

These are formed on the film, upside down and very small – just as images reach the retina in the human eye. The objective lens concentrates the light in the same way as the crystalline lens of the eye.

retina

crystalline

optic nerve

lens

film

Photographic film

This is a thin strip of celluloid, treated on one side with a light sensitive emulsion. It is sold in ready-to-use rolls, disks or cartridges. From this a photographer can obtain 'negatives' and so more copies of the same photographs, or 'positives', for transparency photographs viewed through slides or projectors.

17

LONG DISTANCE COMMUNICATION

Radio, television, radar and the Internet are all systems of long distance communication (telecommunications). In these devices the first signals (sound, images, digital signals) are transformed into electromagnetic waves which are then projected into space by a transmitter. The longest waves, sent back through the atmosphere, are sent to an aerial receiver. This converts the waves back into sounds and images. The shortest waves going through the atmosphere are then bounced back to Earth via satellites. With the telephone and fax machine, electromagnetic waves are usually transmitted through cable.

1894

The first radio transmission

In 1895, the Italian Guglielmo Marconi made the first long-distance transmission of a Morse Code message using radio waves instead of wires, as with the telegraph machine. He called his equipment the 'wire-less' and was soon using it to send messages across seas and continents.

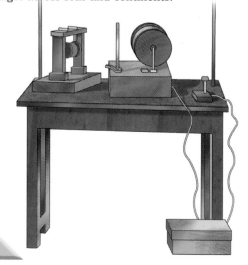

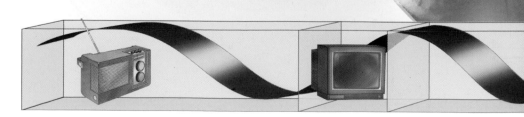

radio waves   TV waves   radar waves

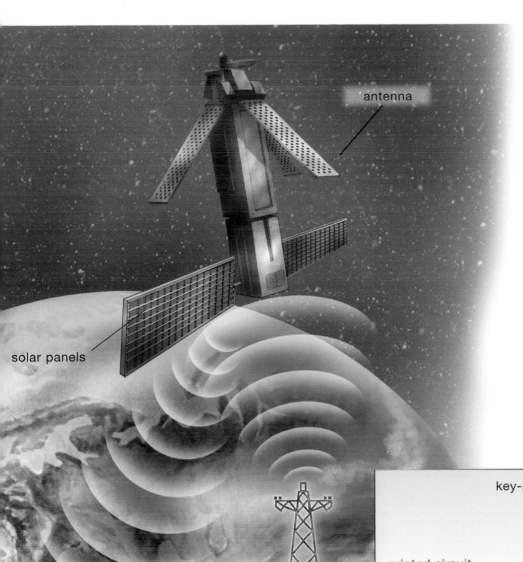

antenna

solar panels

Satellites for communication

In orbit thousands of kilometres above the Earth, artificial satellites relay electromagnetic waves to specific geographical areas of the Earth, each one termed a 'cell'. 66 artificial satellites form a cellular global network which covers the entire surface of the Earth.

Telephone

This device transforms sounds into electrical signals which travel along the cables of a network to a receiver, where they are changed back into sounds. Where there are no cables, signals travel by radio waves. Cellular telephones, without wires, use microwaves.

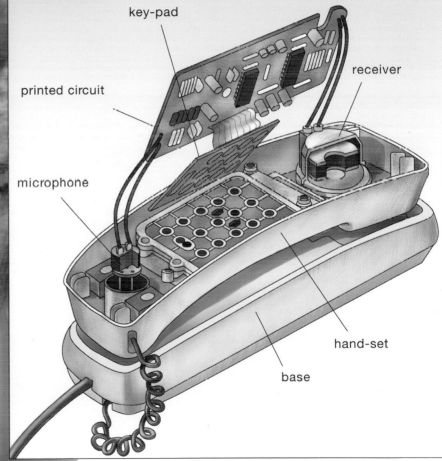

key-pad

printed circuit

receiver

microphone

hand-set

base

Electromagnetic spectrum

This is the name for the complete range of electromagnetic waves which travel through space. These waves are only different by length. The longest waves, such as radio waves, have little energy. Those which are shorter, such as X-rays, have enough energy to pass through matter.

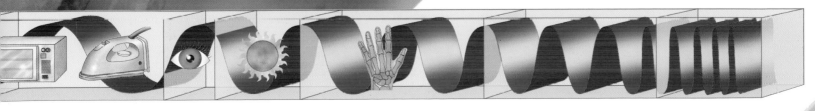

microwaves   infra-red   light waves   ultra-violet   X-rays   Gamma-rays   cosmic-rays

A 'MAGIC' BOX

The television is a system of transmission of images and sound over a distance. The images are captured by television camera and the sounds by a microphone. Images and sounds are relayed as electrical signals to an aerial transmitter. This transforms the signals into electromagnetic waves which are sent into space, and then to a receiver aerial and the television set. The TV converts the signals back into light and sound.

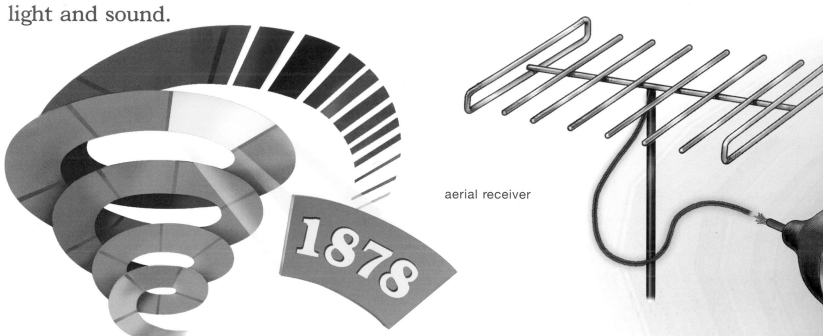

1878

aerial receiver

The cathode-ray tube

This was one of the discoveries which led to the development of television. By 1878, it had been proved that a bottle with the air sucked out would glow when sparks were fired between a metal negative pole (the cathode) to a positive pole (anode). These glowing rays were named 'cathode rays'. In 1912, English physicist J. J. Thomson suggested that these rays were particles of electrons. Then English physicist William Crookes demonstrated that when the cathode rays travel in a straight line to meet at the end of a glass tube, the glass 'lit up' in the form of luminous dots set close together.

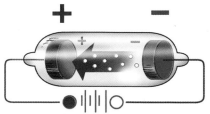

Television set

This is what decodes electrical signals into sounds and images. Each colour is obtained by a different combination of rays produced by cathode-ray tubes, each basic combination corresponding to a colour - blue, red and green.

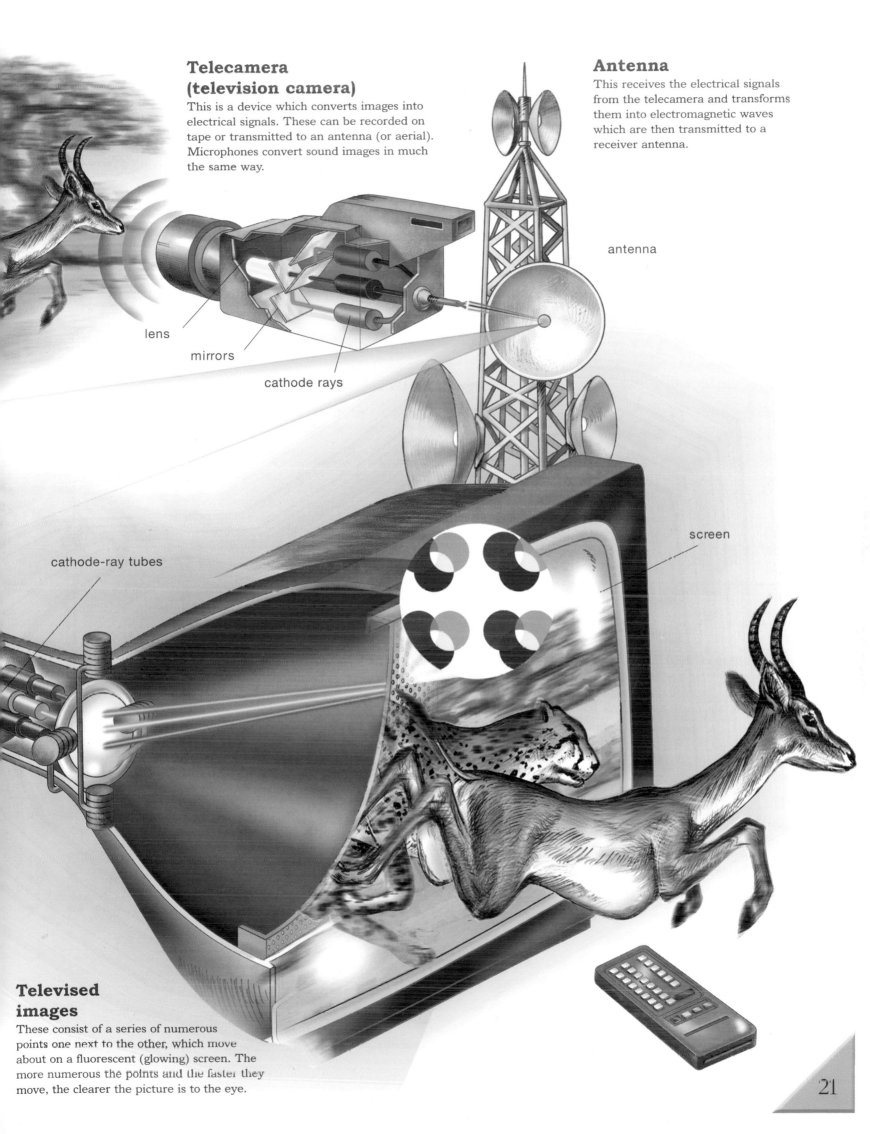

Telecamera (television camera)

This is a device which converts images into electrical signals. These can be recorded on tape or transmitted to an antenna (or aerial). Microphones convert sound images in much the same way.

lens

mirrors

cathode rays

Antenna

This receives the electrical signals from the telecamera and transforms them into electromagnetic waves which are then transmitted to a receiver antenna.

antenna

screen

cathode-ray tubes

Televised images

These consist of a series of numerous points one next to the other, which move about on a fluorescent (glowing) screen. The more numerous the points and the faster they move, the clearer the picture is to the eye.

BOOKS FOR ALL

Before the invention of the printing press, every book had to be written and illustrated by hand, with copies made in the same way. The reproduction of a manuscript took a long time. With the printing press came a much faster production of many copies of a book at a reasonable cost. This has led to the spread of culture, with reasonably-priced editions of the works of great writers, as well as information through the newspapers.

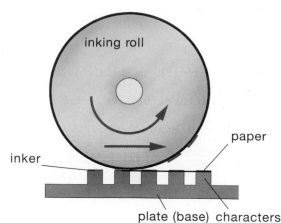

Typographical Press
The characters are raised up on the plate (the base). Ink is transferred directly from the plate to the paper.

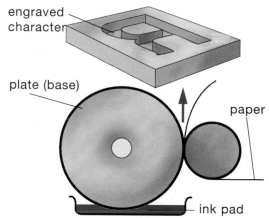

Photogravure (Letter) Press
The characters are engraved by a chemical process on to a rotating copper cylinder, which is fed with ink.

The printing press
This was already being used in 1000 AD by the Chinese who had also made movable 'type' (letters) for the press. However, it was only in 1440 that the German Johann Gutenberg, most probably inspired by presses used to press grapes, built a printing press which exerted a greater pressure on the characters. To compose text, he used movable type in metal, which was more resistant than wood, and gave a better imprint of the printed work.

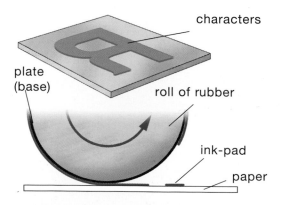

Offset Print (Litho)
The characters are impressed by a special technique on to a metal cylinder, then printed on to paper by means of a roll of rubber.

22

Editing

This is the stage where text and illustrations are prepared for printing. The text is fed into computer and then 'set' or arranged with the illustrations on each page as required. The final result is saved on to floppy disk.

Photo Unit

The floppy disk with the illustrations and the text pass from the editor to the photo-unit. This is an electrical system used to set the text in black and white, and 4-colour or black and white illustrations on to photographic film. This film will then be fed into the printing press.

Photo-Unit

4-colour film for printing

Printing

This is the transfer to paper (or another material) of the characters and the illustrations to be reproduced. In the coloured offset printer, the sheets of paper go through four rollers, each roller fed with ink of a basic colour. By putting one or more colours on top of one another, a whole range of tones is obtained.

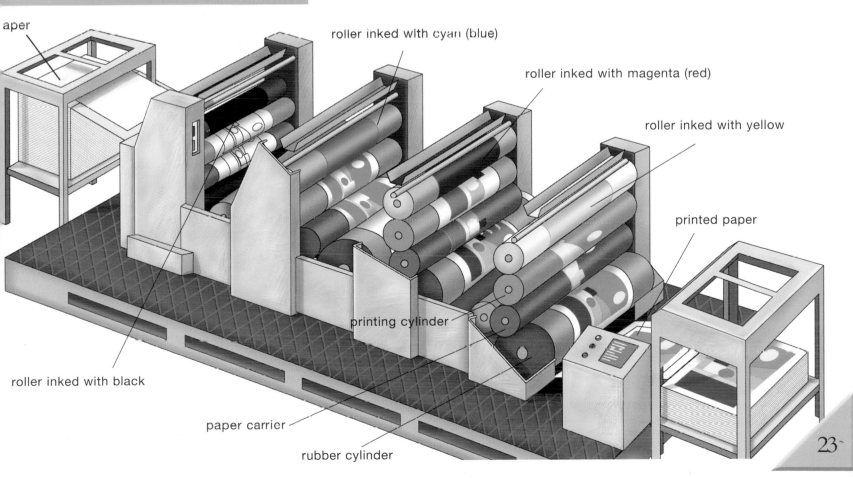

aper

roller inked with cyan (blue)

roller inked with magenta (red)

roller inked with yellow

printed paper

printing cylinder

roller inked with black

paper carrier

rubber cylinder

'INTELLIGENT' MACHINES

In recent years, the computer has revolutionized the way we work and communicate. The computer is an electronic machine which can store and process an enormous quantity of data (information) at high speed. The data which is entered is converted into Binary Code, a special 'computer language' with just two signals – 'on' and 'off' which correspond to 'open' and 'close' an electrical circuit. These two signals are translated as '1' and '0'. Computer memory is measured in 'bytes': one byte is sufficient memory to store one character of data. Using this code, the computer then processes the data and converts it into numbers, letters, illustrations or sounds.

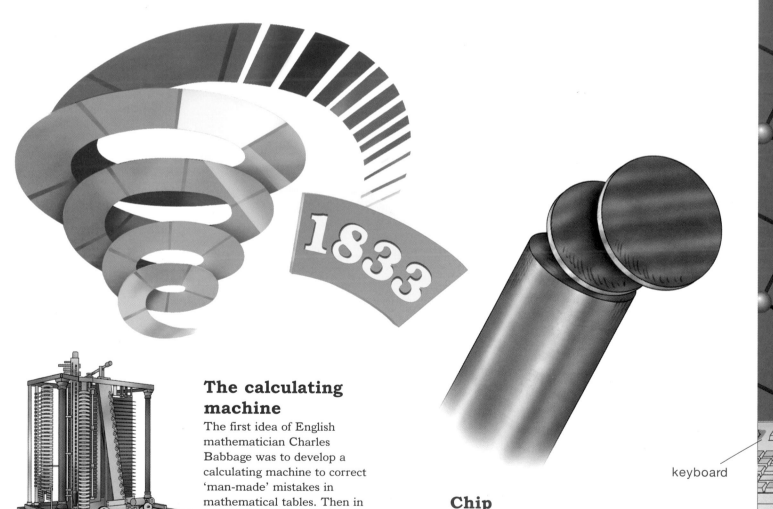

site

keyboard

The calculating machine

The first idea of English mathematician Charles Babbage was to develop a calculating machine to correct 'man-made' mistakes in mathematical tables. Then in 1830 he designed an 'analytical engine' to carry out different mathematical operations and print the results, working on a system of punched cards – the idea which led to the development of the modern computer. Babbage died in 1871, long before his 'analytical engine' was built.

Chip

This is the tiny slice of silicon on which the electronic components in an integrated circuit are stamped.

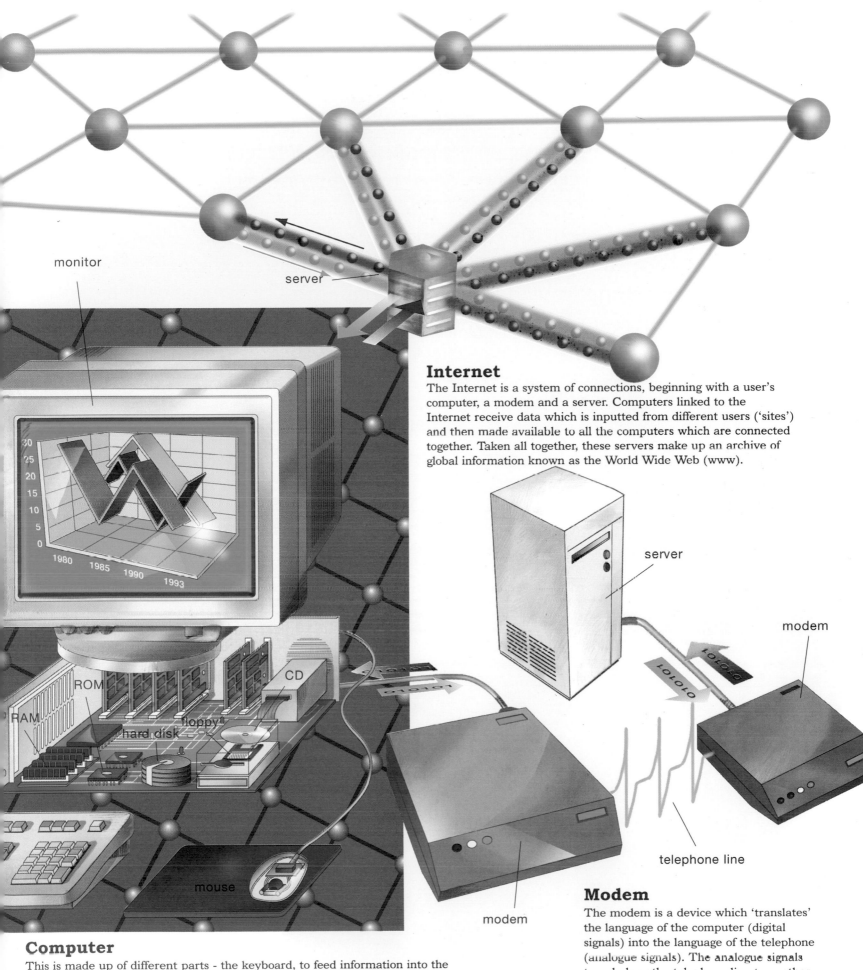

Internet

The Internet is a system of connections, beginning with a user's computer, a modem and a server. Computers linked to the Internet receive data which is inputted from different users ('sites') and then made available to all the computers which are connected together. Taken all together, these servers make up an archive of global information known as the World Wide Web (www).

monitor

server

server

modem

modem

ROM

RAM

floppy

hard disk

CD

mouse

modem

telephone line

Computer

This is made up of different parts - the keyboard, to feed information into the computer, the ROM (Read Only Memory) which stores data and commands, the microprocessor or CPU (Central Processing Unit) which processes the data according to the ROM and then passes it on to the RAM (Random Access Memory). The RAM stores new information and instructions as and when necessary. A monitor shows the different operations on screen. The hard disk (inside the computer), the floppy (portable) disk and a CD all have additional memory to store data.

Modem

The modem is a device which 'translates' the language of the computer (digital signals) into the language of the telephone (analogue signals). The analogue signals travel along the telephone line to another modem, which converts the signals back into digital signals. These signals are received by a central computer (the server) which then distributes the messages to various destinations.

THE PASSAGE OF TIME

Our time is measured both by the rotation of the Earth on its axis and Earth's journey (orbit) around the Sun. One rotation on the Earth's axis takes one day, which can be divided into 24 hours. From ancient times, time has been measured by many different instruments. The sundial is a pole which casts a shadow in different directions according to the time of the day. The hour glass consists of two glass containers, which gives it a shape rather like the letter X. A certain amount of sand takes a measured length of time to pass from one container to the other. But it is the accuracy of the clock which can indicate time with the precision of minutes and seconds.

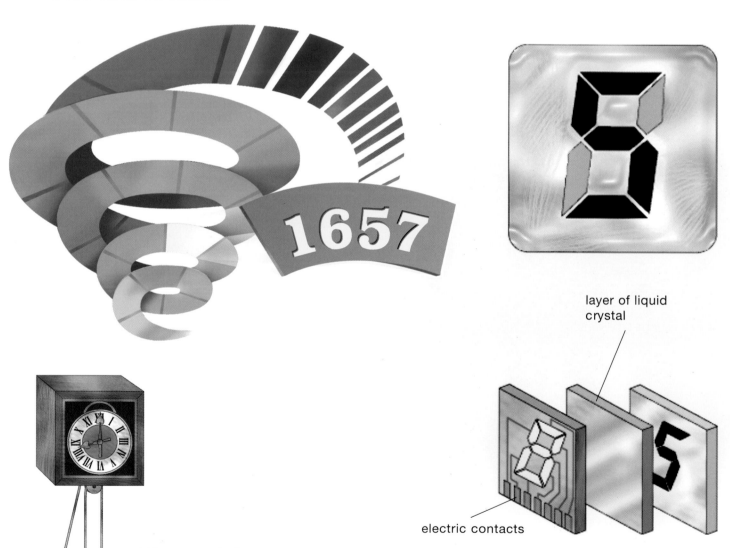

layer of liquid crystal

electric contacts

The pendulum clock
In 1657 the Dutch physicist Christiaan Huygens attached a pendulum (made from a weight attached to a rigid pole) to a clock. The pendulum always took the same time to swing back and forth and so it was possible to measure the movement of the hands with precision.

The digital clock
This shows the time by means of a gadget illuminated by a liquid crystal, a substance which is fluid, like water, but with a well-ordered molecule structure. When activated by electrical current, the crystals change their positions and allow the light to pass through. In this way, the different segments of a 'window' based on the figure 8 are either 'lit up' or 'switched off', in order to show the correct number.

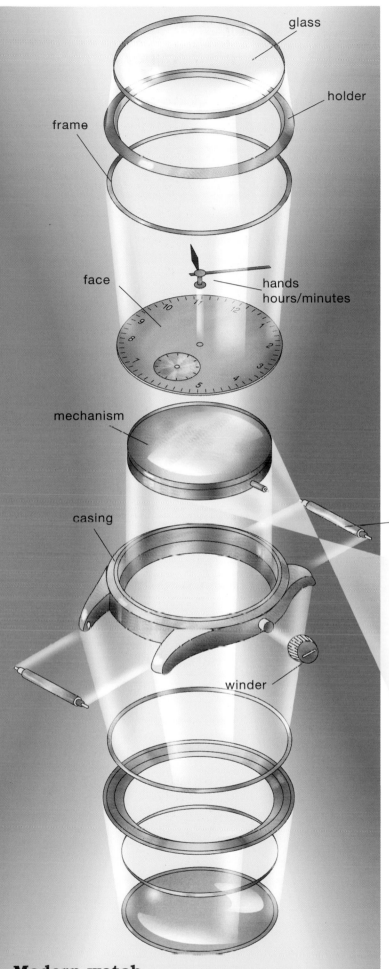

glass

holder

frame

face

hands
hours/minutes

mechanism

casing

holder for a strap

winder

Modern watch

This consists of a mechanism (mechanical or quartz electric)
working from a source of energy (winder or battery) to produce
constant oscillations (back and forth movements) by a balance or
quartz which is connected to an indicator of the hour, minutes and
seconds (hands or digital numbers).

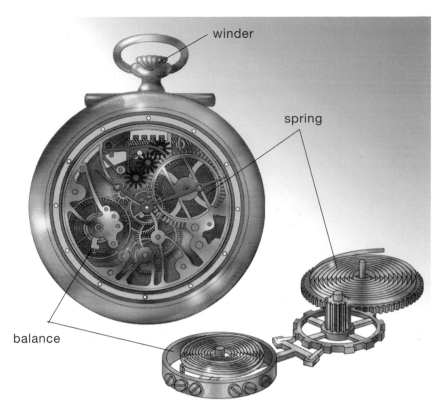

winder

spring

balance

Mechanical watch

This uses the energy released by a spring and is connected by a
series of tooth-edged wheels to the hands. The movement is
regulated by a balance which oscillates regularly forward and back.

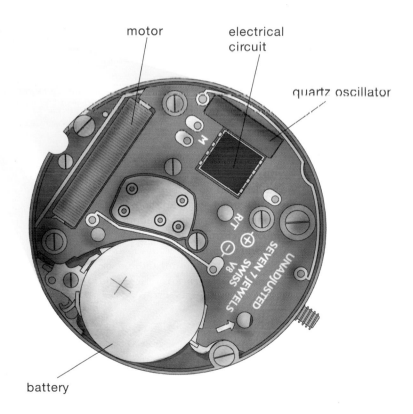

motor

electrical
circuit

quartz oscillator

battery

Quartz watch

This watch uses a battery as a source of energy, which
stimulates a quartz crystal to oscillate in a regular way. An electrical
circuit transforms the oscillations into impulses, one each second,
which are then fed into a tiny motor and this moves the hands.

ANTIBIOTICS AND VACCINES

Medicine was first practised in China up to 2000 BC. Within the last century, it has made great progress, thanks to the study of physiology (the functioning of the human body), bacteriology (the study of micro-organisms which cause illness) and more recently the use of new therapies (methods of cure) which have proved the most effective of all. For instance, vaccination practised on a whole population has almost wiped out certain infectious illnesses, such as diphtheria. The discovery of antibiotics, developed only after the Second World War, has enabled doctors to cure many illnesses which were once fatal.

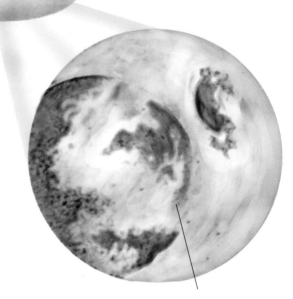

antibiotics

bacteria

1928

dead bacteria cells

Penicillin

In 1928, Scottish bacteriologist Alexander Fleming noticed that a mould of the bacteria Penicillium stopped the growth of some bacteria which he was studying. A substance produced from this mould, penicillin, acted as an antibiotic – that is, it stopped the life of the bacteria. The use of penicillin began in England about 20 years later.

Antibiotics

These are substances which can kill or stop the growth of micro-organisms, such as bacteria, but not viruses. Antibiotics cause the destruction of bacteria cells without harming cells in the human body.

Vaccine

Vaccines are made from the same micro-organisms which cause an illness, but made weaker or inactive, sometimes after having been 'cultivated' in animals. Vaccines are injected into people, with just enough of the micro-organisms for the body to make antibodies to defend itself against the illness, but not enough to cause the illness itself.

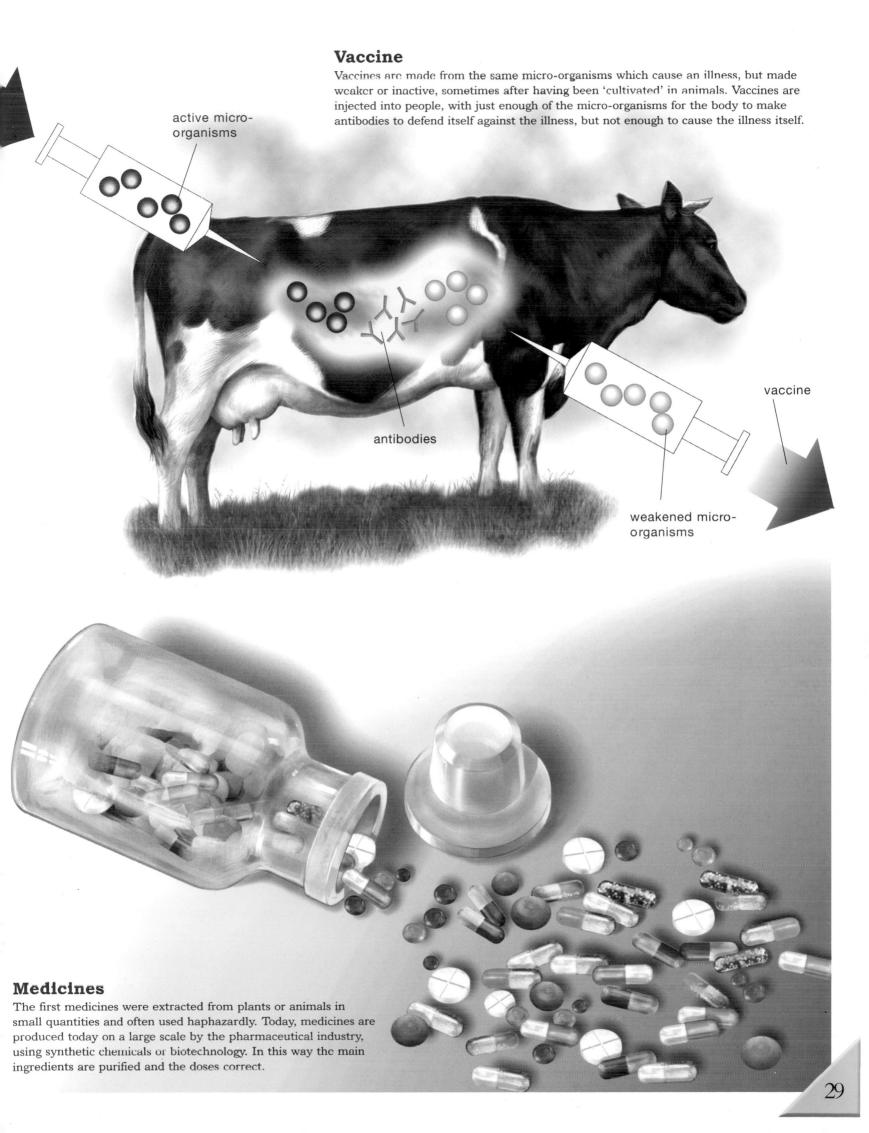

active micro-organisms

antibodies

weakened micro-organisms

vaccine

Medicines

The first medicines were extracted from plants or animals in small quantities and often used haphazardly. Today, medicines are produced today on a large scale by the pharmaceutical industry, using synthetic chemicals or biotechnology. In this way the main ingredients are purified and the doses correct.

'MADE TO MEASURE' ORGANISMS

Biotechnology uses living organisms – cells or parts of cells – to produce useful substances. One biotechnological technique is genetic engineering, where scientists can manipulate or rearrange the genes which are present in all living cells. Genes are passed from parent animals and plants to their young. Each gene has the 'code' to make a set of proteins – the basis of all living cells. By examining the genes in a molecule of DNA, scientists can identify any which may be defective and so be the cause of an illness or defect. By means of genetic engineering, a 'healthy' gene can be transferred from one organism to another, so that plants or animals produce young which are healthier and more resistant to disease.

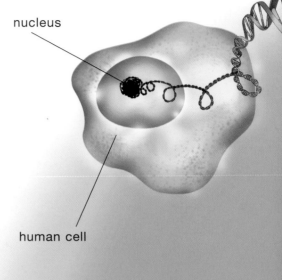

nucleus

human cell

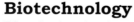

1953–1973

Biotechnology applications

In everyday life - bacteria are 'cultivated' to break down the pollution in waste water.

Biotechnology

Biotechnology has been practised for thousands of years, each time someone uses the live cells of yeast to ferment wine or make dough rise. It was only in the early 20th century that scientists discovered how microscopic fungi (such as yeast) and bacteria live and multiply. The DNA molecule, the basis of modern genetic engineering, was discovered in 1869 by Swiss student chemist Johann Miescher, but he knew little about it. The complete DNA structure was identified in 1953 by biophysicists Francis Crick from England and American, James Watson. Their discovery opened the way for the DNA technique to begin in 1973.

bacteria clones (artificially-produced copies)

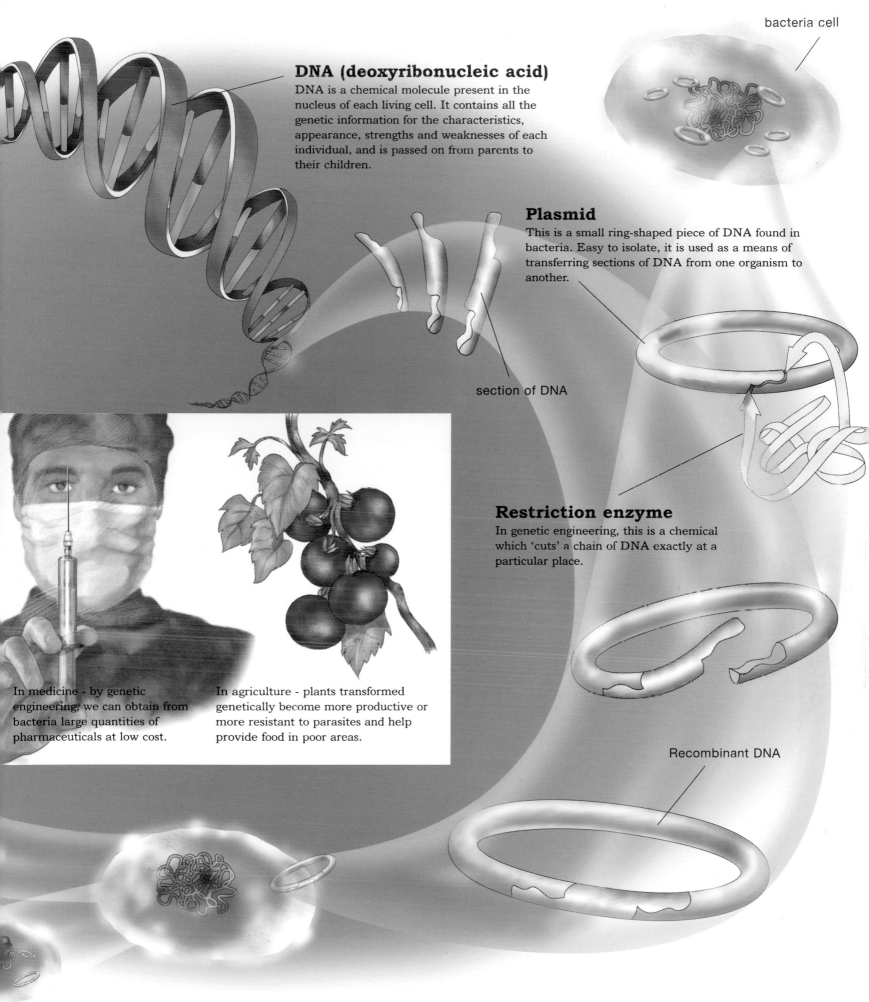

DNA (deoxyribonucleic acid)

DNA is a chemical molecule present in the nucleus of each living cell. It contains all the genetic information for the characteristics, appearance, strengths and weaknesses of each individual, and is passed on from parents to their children.

Plasmid

This is a small ring-shaped piece of DNA found in bacteria. Easy to isolate, it is used as a means of transferring sections of DNA from one organism to another.

section of DNA

Restriction enzyme

In genetic engineering, this is a chemical which 'cuts' a chain of DNA exactly at a particular place.

In medicine - by genetic engineering, we can obtain from bacteria large quantities of pharmaceuticals at low cost.

In agriculture - plants transformed genetically become more productive or more resistant to parasites and help provide food in poor areas.

Recombinant DNA

Recombinant DNA

This is a technique used to modify the genes in a cell. Using a restriction enzyme, a piece of DNA which produces a useful protein is 'cut' from the cell of one organism. This fragment is then transplanted in the plasmid of a bacteria to obtain a 'different' DNA, or a recombinant DNA. The bacteria quickly reproduces, forming many 'clones' (identical cells), and so the fragment of DNA also multiplies. By cloning bacteria, scientists can extract the protein produced by bacteria cells in great quantities.

Glossary

Antenna
A device which can send out or transmit (transmitter antenna) or receive (receiver antenna) electromagnetic waves.

Bacteria
Microscopic organisms, made of only one cell.

Cell
The basis of all living things. There are one-celled organisms, such as bacteria, and living things made up of many cells, such as the human body.

Combustible
A substance which can combine with oxygen to burn and give off heat.

Combustion
A chemical reaction between a combustible substance and the oxygen in the air. Usually gives off a flame and heat.

Electromagnetic spectrum
Collective name for all electromagnetic radiations, including X-rays, light and radio waves.

Electromagnetic waves or radiation
Energy which is transmitted into space in the form of waves. The difference in types of electromagnetic radiation is measured by the length of the wave (the distance between two ends of a wave) and the frequency (the number of waves which are formed within a certain time).

Energy
A power to do work or to work something. One source of energy can be transformed into another – mechanical energy into light energy, electrical energy into heat, etc.

Force
Any cause which changes or modifies the direction or speed of something. For example, a football moves by the muscular force of a leg.

Internal Combustion Engine
An engine which burns fuel inside a cylinder.

Light
A type of electromagnetic radiation which can be perceived by the human eye.

Machine
This can be a simple device (such as a lever) or work with other mechanisms (such as a motor), and which converts energy in order to do a job.

Microwave
A type of electromagnetic radiation. Microwaves are used in the transmission of television programmes and in the microwave oven.

Motor
Any machine which transforms mechanical work (for example, the rotation of a wheel) into other forms of energy (for example, electrical or heat energy).

Pulley
A simple machine made of a wheel or a disc which turns around a pivot supported by a metal stirrup. Used to raise weights.

Radar
An instrument which uses a type of radio wave to determine the position and the speed of movement of an object in space, or the presence of a fixed object.

Radiation
The spreading out of waves or rays from a source of energy - e.g. sunlight, X-rays, microwaves, etc.

Reflection
In optics, this is the phenomenon by which a ray of light is sent back when it hits an object.

Refraction
In optics, it is the phenomenon by which a ray of light is bent when it passes through one transparent substance to another.